Nature Library of Color

DOGS AND PUPPIES

CRESCENT

From the top of its sleek silky head to the tip of its wagging tail the faithful dog of today is an accepted and much loved part of our everyday lives. Man's best friend? Some think so – others are not so sure, but it is undeniably man's oldest, dating right back to the dangerous prehistoric days when it was used by man as a hunting partner and has remained faithfully at his side ever since, devoted and protective. How such a relationship has stood the test of time and not broken up at least once during the thousands of years that man and dog have shared their lives is very much left to speculation. Aldous Huxley said 'To his dog, every man is Napoleon, hence the constant popularity of dogs', while a 19th century American senator touchingly expressed the view – 'The one, absolutely unselfish friend that man can have in this selfish world, the one that never deserts him, the one that never proves ungrateful or treacherous is his dog ... He will kiss the hand that has no food to offer ... When all other friends desert, he remains'. In fiction and in truth the dog has featured prominently in countless tales of courage and unshakable loyalty, often to the extent of forfeiting its own life in order to save its master or mistress from being harmed, and for the lonely it has provided unquestioning friend-ship. It is little wonder then that the dog has, and continues to have, a unique place in our homes and hearts, and few can deny the pleasures of securing such a loving animal as their friend.

Dogs and History

Dogs probably made their presence known before man had even contemplated sharing his life with an animal – a fact often still true today which numerous dog-owners will endorse by telling a tale of the stray that virtually adopted their household and quickly became an important member of the family. But the exact date when the two met and the friendship began is clouded by uncertainty. Always looking for the easiest means by which to obtain food, packs of wild dogs probably prowled around the campsites of the early nomadic hunting tribes, scavenging the carcases that were

(1) and (2) The smallness and vulnerability of puppies makes them almost irresistible. Unfortunately, when puppies grow into dogs, their owners can lose interest and many dogs end up by being thoughtlessly abandoned. (3) The West Highland White Terrier is the only all-white Scottish breed. A native of Argyll, it was originally intended to work the difficult terrain of the Western Highlands. (4) The Golden Retriever is particularly noted for its gentleness, intelligence and willingness to work. As these pages show, there are many types of dog to choose from, and it is worth finding out about them before you do.   4

5

6

7

1

2

4

3

5

6

left to rot after a kill had been made. Apparently less wary of man than other wild animals, these dogs found their way into settlements in their search for food – an act which brought about the first and very successful attempts to domesticate a wild animal. In those early days relationships between man and beast were based on mutual convenience, the struggle to survive was too fierce a one to allow otherwise. Man realised that the dogs possessed far keener senses of hearing and smell than he did and were able to detect more quickly the presence of dangerous predators outside the camp. Not long after, wild dogs were used to hunt down game and trap it, waiting for man to arrive and make the kill. But despite this, the growth of affection was a gradual one. The more gentle dogs of the pack were probably the only ones to be tolerated in the camps and others were killed for food or driven out. It is possible that man hand-reared some of the early puppies to produce a less ferocious dog, whose increasing dependence on him made it easier to derive good and safe usage from the animal. When man eventually

(1) Graceful and aristocratic Afghan Hound.
(2) Great Dane.
(3) to (7) All these puppies, whatever the breed, have almost pleading expressions which, combined with their floppy ears and cuddly bodies cannot fail to appeal.
(8) Golden Cocker Spaniel.
(9) The long-haired Old English Sheepdog is strong, very active and makes an ideal family pet.

Overleaf: *Three enchanting Corgi pups. The origins of these little dogs are vague but it is likely that they are related to the cattle-dog mentioned in the old laws of Wales codified in 920 AD. Today Corgis are known throughout the world and, helped no doubt by royal patronage, have become increasingly popular family pets.*

discovered the convenience of keeping herds of wild animals in captivity to provide a constant food source, dogs were used to protect the animals and trained to round up the herds and keep them together when it was necessary to move from one grazing area to another. No doubt even at this point if food was scarce man had no hesitation in killing his dogs to eat them – an act which would find little sympathy in the modern world – and if the dog became sufficiently starved it would equally have quickly turned on man.

This mutual and largely beneficial association grew stronger over the years and gradually changed into the real affection that it is today. Man and dog would be lonely and lost without each other.

History of Different Breeds

The wild relatives of the dog include wolves, jackals and foxes, and all belong to a single species known as Canis Familiaris. It is not accurately known which animal is the dog's major ancestor but the popular belief is that it is descended from the grey wolf which roamed the plains of Europe, Asia and North America, and pictures on the walls of early man's caves show that the original hunting dog bore a strong resemblance to the wolf. The Australian Dingo is the only surviving breed that has maintained many of the early physical characteristics. However, three major features distinguish dogs from their wild relatives. They are to be found in countries all over the world; the structure of their mouths and tails have developed differently; and genetically, due to man's own design, there is an enormous amount of variability – from the Irish Wolfhound, which may stand as high as thirty-nine inches at the shoulder – to the small breeds. The tiniest recorded is a Yorkshire Terrier which stood three-and-a-half inches high and weighed only ten ounces as an adult. Shape, size, colour and temperament vary

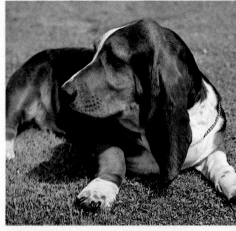

Dogs are usually thought to be intelligent. One fact that gives rise to this assumption is that they are generally trainable, obedient and capable of learning to perform tricks on demand. Alertness is a quality to look for when choosing a dog, but this should not be confused with aggressiveness or hysteria.

1

3

2

4

tremendously and there are dogs with long silky hair or short, fluffy hair; floppy-eared ones and those whose ears are pricked up and alert. There are even a few breeds, such as the Mexican hairless, that are, as their name suggests, entirely without hair.

It was, in fact, man who produced all these different breeds. When traders sailed to other countries it was discovered that other dogs already existed, each specially adapted to its environment, displaying a variety of attributes that proved advantageous to man. He cross-bred to exaggerate certain qualities and quickly developed a range of dogs, each specifically designed for a purpose. So rapidly did the different breeds emerge that the Romans devised a system of classi-

fication with the following categories: shepherd dogs, house dogs, war dogs, scent dogs, those that hunted by sight, and sporting dogs. Today classification varies from country to country.

Two distinct groups exist amongst the hunting breeds – those that use their sight and speed to hunt and those that track down their game by the scent in the air and on the ground.

The Basset Hound (8) is a lively and amusing companion. Despite its short legs, it in fact has the body of a large dog and consequently needs a lot of exercise. Bassets used to be kept for hunting hares.
The Pyrenean Mountain Dog (2) is a wise and dignified creature. It was originally used as a guardian to flocks and herds in mountain pastures and its gentle nature makes it particularly good with children.

Archaelogical excavations have revealed that greyhounds, also called gazehounds, featured prominently in Ancient Egypt. Their powers as hunters are best suited to hot, dry climates where it is difficult to pick up scents, but the wide open spaces make visibility excellent. These dogs are easily recognisable by their long, slender limbs and slim bodies forming a high arch at the loins. Their greatest asset is their speed, and today they are popular in Britain and America where greyhound racing is a well-liked sport and also big business. A much larger dog is portrayed in early Assyrian frescoes. This dog, which looked very much like the modern mastiff, was used on the battlefield and to hunt lions. It is probable that all these Middle Eastern breeds were brought to Europe by Phoenician traders who sailed over to buy tin from the Cornish tin mines.

The majority of the scent hounds have a history which goes equally as far back in time. The bright-eyed and alert beagle, made famous by that lovable cartoon character 'Snoopy', is particularly popular in Britain where packs are used to hunt foxes and hares. The droopy basset hound, notorious for its soulful expression and lazy ways, is actually an excellent hunter and was used by the French to hunt small forest animals and by the police to track down criminals.

Sporting dogs – spaniels, retrievers, setters, labradors and pointers, bred to 'fetch and carry', do not actually assist in the killing of an animal. The pointer does exactly what its name suggests. It is thought to have originated in Spain and its powers of sight and smell, speed and stamina are all equally well developed, making it a good all-round field dog. Spaniels do not lead their handlers to the game but have been bred, by the British, to flush a bird out of hiding and then find it and bring it to the feet of the handler after the shoot. Labradors and retrievers too have been bred to sit by their masters' feet until the bird has been shot and then find it and pick it up. Labradors originally came from the coast of Newfoundland where they accompanied fishermen out to sea in the 19th century, assisting with the carrying of the

There are almost one hundred different types of hound including the Basset (3) and the Bloodhound (7). The Bloodhound is self-willed and has the best scenting powers of any breed of dog. Its features are highly distinctive and its smooth coat can be tan, red-brown or black-and-tan. The breed is descended from animals brought into England by William the Conquerer and it has been used for hunting red deer, as a patrol dog, and as a tracking dog by the Police.

1

2

3

4

5

6

9

mooring rope from the boat to the shore and rescuing anything that fell overboard while at sea.

It was realised early on how good a companion a dog could be in the home and as far back as the Kingdom of Ancient Egypt small dogs, which are now known as the Toy breeds, were developed as pets. The Chinese also bred small, flat-faced dogs, the first of which to reach the West was the pug, which became a fashionable court dog in the 16th and 17th centuries. Miniature poodles, very popular and often over-pampered pets, only date back to the beginning of the 20th century, although the origins of the standard poodle lie considerably further back in time. The Pekinese, a firm favourite all over the world, was bred in China in the 8th century and is a member of the spaniel family.

The reason that such good historical records exist of the emergence of the majority of breeds is because they all attracted the interest of artists and historians. The working breeds, it seems, did not. All have been in existence for centuries and today some are still used for their original functions and make fine family pets but little is known of their appearance before the 19th century. The Pyrenean mountain dog, in its time used as a guard dog and a war dog, is exceptionally beautiful and the collies, well known as sheep dogs, display an uncanny ability to reason out the most difficult situations when rounding up flocks of sheep. The popular and plucky Yorkshire terrier was originally used for ratting in the woollen factories and the 'huskies', a name which encompasses a wide variety of breeds, still pull sleds in the Arctic and Antarctic where temperatures frequently fall to minus fifty. In Europe, even today, a milk float can occasionally be seen drawing slowly past, pulled by a large golden retriever-like dog called the leonberger, and the magnificent Bernese mountain dog was a popular Swiss haulage animal.

The distinctive wrinkled face of the Bulldog (2) makes it very easy to identify. Its severe frown belies a gentle nature. Its appearance is a result of generations of careful breeding but the somewhat unnatural structure of the animal's head can lead to health problems – especially breathing difficulties, and the dogs often wheeze.

In the Home

There are many reasons for people choosing to own pets and more still explaining why some choose cats, some dogs and others rabbits or hamsters. A lonely person can derive great comfort from keeping a dog and may feel safer with such an alert and reliable guard protecting the house. Lazy people who feel that they really ought to get some exercise will find that a dog is a great incentive to go out for long walks in the country and others simply need to love and care for another being, with the assurance that the affection will not be criticised or rejected.

A dog in its natural environment is used to being a member of a pack and obeying the laws laid down by the leader. In the home it is this sort of relationship with its owner which will bring out the best in it. It expects to be disciplined and a dog-owner must have sufficient authority to command

The Yellow Labrador (1) and (5) probably originated in Newfoundland where its forebears are thought to have been water dogs – swimming between boats and shore carrying whatever was required of them. The Labrador is a popular and widespread breed although its Newfoundland ancestors are almost extinct.
Looking at these pictures, it is not hard to understand man's love for his four-legged friends, and the most extraordinary bond of loyalty that frequently exists between the two!

6

7

the dog's respect – anything other than this will probably result in a very temperamental dog. Its basic needs are simple but demanding. Unlike a cat, a dog is not equipped for an independent life. If it is going to be left on its own for long periods of time another animal would probably be a better choice. The more time a dog is allowed to spend with its owner, and the more it is involved in the general activities that are going on in the house, the happier it will be.

The basics of dog-ownership are of vital importance. Naturally the amount of food it is necessary to buy varies according to the size of the dog, but care must be taken with the diet of all dogs and this will be an expense. They will also need to be treated by a vet from time to time and, unless a good friend can look after them well during holidays, boarding accommodation will have to be found. If the thought of muddy paw marks and hairs on the carpet does not appeal, for instance to those who wish their house kept in immaculate condition, again a dog would not be the ideal pet, and if there will not be the time (or the inclination) to give the animal sufficient exercise, perhaps a hamster would be better.

To try to describe the personality of dogs is an impossibility. Anybody who has known more than one dog will know that to generalise about any one breed, other than its physical characteristics, would be misleading, let alone the whole of the domestic canine population. If looked after well and given sufficient attention, all dogs will be devoted companions – that is for certain – and very few dogs have a miserable outlook on life. Usually they will be full of joy and eager to participate in family affairs. But there the similarities end; understandably so, for how could a massive St Bernard have a nature comparable to that of the tiny chihuahua. Coupled with its own individual personality, the character of any one dog will also depend to a large extent on the environment it is brought up in. A happy, carefree household full of easy-going people will probably have a dog that, as an adult, whatever its breed, has a similar approach to life.

If treated properly, whatever the inherent traits of the particular breed,

Jack Russell Terriers (7) are not recognised as a breed by the Kennel Club and therefore are not shown in competitions – although this by no means diminishes their popularity as family pets.
This group of four Blue Roan Cocker Spaniel pups (1) would be a delightful adornment to any box of chocolates!

5

6

7

8

every dog will have a sweet and loving nature and will be prepared to do almost anything that it thinks pleases its master or mistress.

The Senses

In 1925 a Dobermann pinscher called Sauer, who belonged to a South African police force, is said to have followed, and found, a thief over a distance of some one hundred miles by scent alone. We have about five million receptor cells in our nasal membranes as opposed to 220 million in the best tracker dog. To many dogs, using their nose is the major way of forming an effective picture of their environment and, combined with their hearing ability which is also highly developed, their awareness of their surroundings is far greater than ours. In social relations these acute senses are of utmost importance. Dogs mark their territory with urine and a bitch on heat will know there is a male nearby simply by smelling it. The smell will also be a warning to other males to keep away. When two dogs first meet they sniff each other to establish friendship, or the fact that they don't like each other. Sniffing the clothes, hands and face of their owner speaks volumes about where the person has been and it also makes it easier to identify someone who has only visited the house once or twice before. Taste is closely associated

Irish or Red Setters (1) are the descendents of a mediaeval hunting dog – the Setting Spaniel – which was trained to find birds and then 'set' (i.e. crouch down) so that a net could be thrown over dog and birds. The dog can be extremely flighty and energetic and is not the easiest of pets to keep.

Overleaf: West Highland White Terriers.

with smell in most mammals but, in general, dogs have fewer taste buds than we do. Like all carnivores, once a dog has sniffed its food to find out whether it likes it or not, it will swallow it virtually whole, discriminating little between the flavour of various components.

The acute sense of hearing that dogs possess is of great advantage to an owner. Dogs respond well to training, mainly because they quickly learn to associate a sound with a resulting action – good or bad. The vocabulary that exists between a

human and a dog is therefore extremely individual, because it is up to the owner which sounds will signify food, walk and so on, and not an existing vocabulary that humans have to learn. It is commonly accepted that dogs respond to the tone of a voice and not to what is actually being said. People with very monotonous voices often have more difficulty in training their dogs than those with naturally fluctuating voices, especially women, whose voices are pitched at a higher frequency which most animals respond to more readily. Sometimes, if a particular record is played on a gramophone a dog will start howling,

The Alsatian or German Shepherd Dog (1) and (3) came into existence in its present form less than one hundred years ago, when Rittmeister von Stephanitz supervised the inter-breeding of three ancient strains of European shepherd dog. The attractive and intelligent result has become world famous, starring in several films and proving to be an invaluable asset to the police forces and armed forces everywhere.

8

9

10

1

2

3

4

which some people credit to enjoyment but others say is because the dog's ears are so sensitive that the combination of frequencies are actually hurting it. A breed which has naturally pricked up ears will almost certainly have more acute hearing than one with large, floppy ears, which will depend even more on its sense of smell.

How good any one dog's sight will be depends largely on the breed. The structure of a dog's eyes restricts the movement of the eyeballs in the sockets and they are positioned to look straight ahead. This is compensated for by most dogs having a very mobile neck and moving their heads often. Until recently it was thought that dogs, like cats, could only see in black and white, but now it is known that they have faint colour vision, although nowhere near as highly developed as ours. Sight is sharpest in working dogs and sporting dogs, and gundogs specifically bred for retrieving game are almost entirely dependent on vision for their job. A blind dog, however, does not seem to lose its sense of direction or retrieving ability and an owner can be unaware for quite a while that a dog is losing its sight.

Intelligence

Most owners will claim their own dog is a highly intelligent animal and will no doubt come up with some little anecdote as proof. Dogs are easily trained, sometimes to a very high standard, which partly explains why people have this notion that they are intelligent. Scientists, however, are always quick to deny any theory which suggests than an animal, other than man, possesses intelligence, saying that tricks are learnt by what is called operant conditioning, whereby if one action is performed it will directly or indirectly cause a change in the animal's surroundings, and therefore the animal will continue to do it if the result if favourable and cease if it is not. Intelligence can be defined in a number of ways, one of which is the ability to intellectually recognise and solve a problem and quickly react physically in order to put it right. Is it not therefore intelligence when a dog works out how to turn a handle to open a door and allow itself into a certain room? Certainly to watch a

Snowy-white Samoyed pups (5) are often nicknamed 'Smiling Dogs'. Their beautiful coats need thorough and regular grooming, and a healthy Samoyed will require a good deal of exercise. The breed has been successfully used as guard dog and sled dog.

The Collie (3) is a highly intelligent and energetic creature, and is highly prized as a Scottish sheep-herding dog. If kept as a family pet, this dog again needs a lot of exercise – at least an hour a day, as well as regular grooming to keep its long coat soft and tangle-free.

sheep dog at trials, rounding up sheep often under difficult circumstances leaves little doubt that these dogs have an ability to solve a problem patiently and effectively, a problem which would have utterly defeated the majority of humans.

Not only is it difficult to ascertain how intelligent dogs are in comparison to man but also which are the smarter breeds of dogs. Providing incentive is an important factor in getting a dog to do anything, and extensive study of various breeds shows that there does not appear to be any substantial difference in the intellectual capacity of dogs, whatever their breed. Many people think that pedigrees are automatically less intelligent than mongrels but there is very little evidence to support this idea – particularly as there are numerous examples of extremely bright pure breds throughout the country and equally as many slow mongrels.

Humans vary in their mental abilities and there is no reason why animals should be different in this respect. Certain intellectual limitations obviously exist for dogs; they cannot talk for instance, but certain breeds do lend themselves to more complex training than others and are therefore

As with horses, there are special terms used when describing the colour of a dog's coat: a blue-grey coat is known as merle, a deep chestnut colour is called red, brindle is light beige with darker hairs intermingled and tricolour as the word implies, is three colours – usually black, white and tan.

thought to be more intelligent. A well trained dog can be so responsive to its owner's every move that it almost seems to read the owner's mind.

Communication

Even though domestication has required that dogs make themselves understood by their human companions, as well as by their canine colleagues, many of their actions are governed by instinct. Dogs communicate with each other by body language and scent. A variety of facial expressions and general postures which may appear quite basic convey a great deal about their desires and emotions. It must be assumed that no animal has such a complex means of verbal communication as we do but it is often the tongue that covers up a multitude of basic instincts in our society, which other animals continue to follow without fear, doubt or shame. Of course dogs have perfectly good vocal chords which, as everybody knows, work much too well on occasions. Dogs bark when excited and happy or when uncertain and questioning. Small dogs are renowned for yapping a lot but larger, working dogs are considerably quieter and it can often come as quite a surprise to hear a loud, booming bark from one of them. Whining reveals that a dog is uncomfortable or slightly perturbed and aggression is conveyed by a growl, often very menacing, especially when accompanied by the lips being drawn back and the teeth bared.

When two dogs meet each other, tail carriage is usually a good indication, to each other and to their owners, whether it is going to be a friendly encounter or not. If one is nervous it will approach slightly crouched with its tail held well down between its legs, a position which will also be adopted if a dog is out of favour with its master or mistress. Two male dogs, especially if they are

King Charles Spaniels (4) owe their name to King Charles I who was particularly fond of the breed – and many portraits of the monarch feature them. These spaniels are characterised by their charming snub-noses and winsome round eyes. Those featured here display black-and-tan colouring, but the most popular are probably the red-and-white.

6

of equal standing, will approach each other rigidly alert, muscles taught and tails held high, ready to be friendly but equally open to a fight, when the hackles will rise and a bloodcurdling snarl will signify the starting point.

A dog intensely dislikes being made to feel that it has done something wrong, especially if it knows full well that it has. No dog is devious by nature and it will convey unhappiness by the mere look in its eyes, as well as the sad posture it adopts. The moment it is forgiven, its tail, whether short, long, fluffy or cropped will madly wag in every direction with pure delight. Puppies are particularly easy to understand. Big, watery eyes, always inquisitive, reflect surprise at every new thing that is discovered. They will jump visibly at strange noises and prick up their ears in an exaggerated attempt to grasp the story that surrounds every sound. Pleasure, pain, unhappiness and fear are all emotions that are easily identified in any puppy.

But what of the way we communicate with them? Do they understand our language or are the scientists who say that it is only tone of voice that is understood by dogs, right? Many are the stories that disprove their theories. A young Labrador who lives in a house where the occupants speak a variety of languages not only understands the word 'walk' in English, Italian and French, whoever the word is spoken by, but gets equally excited and rushes for his lead when the word is spelt out 'W-A-L-K.' He also runs to the window to look fervently at the trees outside if anybody so much as mention the word 'squirrel' in passing. Perhaps one day, somebody will prove whether or not animals can understand our language, but until then we will have to be content with our own opinions.

Courtship

Many delightful cartoons depict dogs living their lives as humans do and 'courting' their lady friends. While she languishes at home, painting her toenails and making herself pretty, numerous dogs draw up outside in various cars, displaying different degrees of wealth and charm in an

2

Poodles (6) are popular, friendly little dogs of great character and individuality. Their coats need regular grooming, and, as they do not shed their fur like other dogs, they need to be clipped. You can easily do this yourself, but if you wish for a special appearance, take the dog to a professional.

3

4

5

6

7

1

2

3

4

5

6

attempt to secure her hand in marriage. What a strange sight this would be if it were the case. In natural conditions a dog is attracted by the smell of a bitch on heat and, as with most animals, courtship preliminaries are very few. However, a dog will show his interest in a bitch, cocking his head mischievously to one side and inviting her to play games, even though he may get nowhere if the bitch has not reached full oestrus and therefore is not ready to mate. Once receptive, the bitch allows the dog to mount her and the pair remain locked together for about twenty minutes, sometimes for as long as an hour.

9

This little creature (9) looks more like a teddy-bear than a dog! It is in fact a Chow Chow pup. In its native land, China, it was at one time eaten, as well as being a hunter and a watchdog. Another dog with a Chinese background is the Pekingese (6), named after the capital, Peking, where it was kept for many hundreds of years as a court dog. Nowadays, these pretty little dogs are among the most popular of household pets.

Family Life

In human terms a successful family includes both mother and father looking after their children. In the animal kingdom this is the exception rather than the rule. The female dog is fully equipped to bring up the puppies on her own and more often than not she will never see the father again. The gestatory period is usually 63 days and the pups are born at an early stage of development. The size of the litter varies not only according to the breed but to the individual bitch. It is usually two or more and sometimes as many as twelve

8

puppies that make up a litter. The highest number ever recorded was 23. In the wild, whelping and rearing take place naturally, without complications, but the further away the domestic dog moves from the shape of its ancestor and the lifestyle it was subject to in the wild, the greater the likelihood is of problems occurring during whelping. Some of the very inbred Toy breeds do not seem to have sufficient strength to give birth unaided whilst breeds such as the Boston Bull Terrier and the Pekingese also have difficulty in delivering because their hips are so narrow. If the birth follows a normal pattern the mother will clean off the membrane after each puppy appears, biting through the umbilical cord, eating the afterbirth and licking each puppy clean and dry. Finding a nipple from which to suck some nourishing milk is every puppy's first reaction. The puppies are born virtually helpless, with eyes and ears tightly closed and very little fur on their bodies. For the first day or two the mother will stay with them for the majority of the time, keeping them warm, safe and well-fed, but later, when she leaves them alone for short periods, they will huddle together for warmth. It is not long though before the eyes and ears start to open, perhaps ten to fourteen days, and the puppies tentatively start to wander away from their mother for short spells. After about three to four weeks the puppies show signs of independence and the mother begins to detach herself from the litter, although she will be quick to help any pups in difficulty. The puppies will start trying to eat solid food but they will not be fully weaned until six to eight weeks of age. To teach them self-sufficiency the mother disciplines them prudently, cuffing them for any misbehaviour and teaching them to keep the sleeping basket clean. She will also encourage and join in their play which is a vital way for them to

Most dogs nowadays are fed commercially-produced tinned food. The dog gulps its food with little or no chewing but its teeth do need to be used. There is probably nothing a dog likes better than a large uncooked bone to gnaw – do not give a dog cooked bone as these tend to splinter and can get caught in the animal's throat. Another source of exercise for the teeth is hard, crunchy dog biscuits – large enough not to be swallowed whole! The biscuits will also provide essential roughage.

learn the skills that will be required of them in adult life. The ideal time to sell a litter or to become the proud owner of a puppy is believed to be when it has acquired the maturity and independence of spirit that comes with being a full eight weeks old.

Puppy Power

Puppies are totally irresistible. At only three to four weeks old all the charm that we normally associate with these little creatures will cast its spell over dog-lovers and non dog-lovers alike, and for a while a puppy cannot put a paw wrong. In reality, a puppy's appeal can wear rather thin at times. Away for the first time from its littermates at about two months old, locked in the kitchen or a pen in a big house at night it will yelp continually for a while, soil the floor and chew its way through anything and everything that it can get its small but sharp little teeth into. Fortunately however, a puppy can soon be persuaded that a morsel of meat is far tastier than a slipper, that daytimes are much more fun if you actually sleep at night and confine singing practice to the daylight hours and that the nice green patch of grass outside the back door is much more suitable for relieving oneself than the thick pile carpet in the living room.

The following weeks, during which the puppy will be growing and finding out about the world inside the house and, after it has been inoculated by the vet, outside, will be pure delight. The occasion is so memorable that it more often than not finds its way into many family photo albums and is still brought up in conversation many years later. Everything will be of interest to a puppy and if you would rather not have something investigated by a damp, olive-black nose and probing paws, it is best to put it out of the way where it cannot be found. Not only will a puppy try to get into and on top of anything possible, but it will also try to eat it – except, sometimes, the food you put before it. Love and affection shown to it will be amply returned and it will become devoted

A serene portrait of three Collies.

to its owner and probably the whole family very early on. Its apparent concern for your cleanliness as it licks you all over every time you walk into the room is extremely touching and the look you will receive from it as it sits on the shirt that had been carefully ironed and laid out for wear that evening will convince you that it is definitely for your own good that it is doing this. The shirt probably didn't suit you anyway.

Owning a puppy is therefore a time of great joy. Unfortunately all too often it is the puppy's irresistible nature which brings about its downfall. Too many puppies are bought on impulse as Christmas and birthday presents without any thought being given to the implications of owning a

dog. It is often not known how big a mongrel puppy will eventually grow and even if the puppy is a pedigree and the eventual size and personality can be estimated, the amount of care, affection and basic floor space that any dog will eventually require is quite considerable. Many people are not prepared for this and yet still buy a puppy, thoughtlessly turning it out when it is unsuitable for their home. A great deal of thought should therefore go into not only whether to

Terriers (1) and (5) are sturdy, courageous dogs. The name – terrier – derives from 'terra' meaning earth in Latin and these dogs were originally used to hunt foxes and badgers, driving or digging them out of holes in which they had gone to earth.
In complete contrast to the terrier is the Saint Bernard (4), a huge, kindly-looking dog. The breed is probably descended from the mastiff-like dogs which the Romans introduced to Europe from Asia. These dogs are renowned as pathfinders and rescuers and have saved many lives, particularly in the Swiss Alps.

6

7

8

Large or small, long-legged or squat, smooth coated or rough – dogs in all their shapes and sizes are a constant source of delight. Man never grows tired of the companionship that these animals have to offer – indeed, who could resist the unquestioning adulation that a dog bestows upon its master or mistress? Not merely companionship, but friendship too, and a strength of loyalty which has resulted in many instances of dogs risking their lives to save a beloved master or mistress – and vice versa! The dog's unquestioning faithfulness will always be there regardless of what the rest of the world thinks, and to your dog, you are the most important being in that world.

1

2

3

4

7

5

6

purchase a puppy in the first place, but also which breed to buy, for which sound advice can be sought from breeders. If a puppy is bought, register it with the local vet and find out what innoculations must be administered; how often a booster will be needed, and seek expert advice on basic health care and how to provide it with a good, balanced diet. If a puppy is treated correctly it will remain a faithful and devoted companion for the rest of its life.

Training

Many breeds of dog can be trained to a very high standard and will perform remarkable tricks, but most dog-owners are happy to teach their dog the basics, for its own safety when crossing roads, to avoid having the neighbourhood brand it as a public nuisance because it runs riot in a busy street, and also to gain a sense of pride from owning such a well-behaved animal. It is commonly thought to be the mark of a good, authoritative owner and it is in a

Despite its sometimes alarming appearance, the Boxer (8) is generally extremely good-natured, often a real softie! It is a strong active and energetic animal and it needs a lot of exercise. The breed is of German origin and it was developed to provide guard dogs and police dogs. To achieve the most potential from a Boxer, it needs to be carefully and patiently trained. In Britain, Boxers' ears are not cropped, a tradition which is practised elsewhere. The fun-loving Boxer is an ideal companion for an energetic owner!
Another dog which requires a lot of exercise is the elegant Saluki (2). A member of the Greyhound family, it is one of the oldest of the world's hunting dogs.

relatively strict environment, where a dog knows its place and has rules to obey, that it is at its happiest and most secure. Martha Scott said "Don't make the mistake of treating your dogs like humans, or they'll treat you like dogs." A dog must be taught to fit in with its owner's way of life and it is therefore to man's advantage that its natural instincts make it easy to train. There is little evidence to suggest that a smarter dog makes it more susceptible to training. Indeed it can often work the other way round, whereby an intelligent and perceptive dog quickly learns what it can get away with not

doing and may be more difficult to train as a result. Most problems arise from a clash of personalities. As with humans, the degree of dominance and submissiveness varies enormously in the canine world – in the wild the dog is a pack animal and is given an order of precedence based on strength and natural dominance which is strictly adhered to by each member of the pack. Not only do the subordinate dogs fear and

When you have made your choice, and the time comes to collect your puppy, it is worth remembering that the animal is facing one of the most traumatic occasions in its whole life. It is leaving the only home it has known, and the warmth and comfort of its family. Have a cosy bed waiting – somewhere safe where the animal can hide from prying eyes. A hot water bottle – well wrapped – will be a good substitute for mother's warmth.

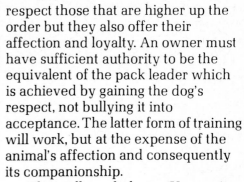

respect those that are higher up the order but they also offer their affection and loyalty. An owner must have sufficient authority to be the equivalent of the pack leader which is achieved by gaining the dog's respect, not bullying it into acceptance. The latter form of training will work, but at the expense of the animal's affection and consequently its companionship.

The well-used phrase 'You can't teach an old dog new tricks' is to a large extent true. Once a dog has matured and is set in its ways, it will not be an easy task to show it something new and expect it to learn. It is far better to train a puppy so that

One of the most heart-rending sounds a new dog-owner has to bear, is the plaintive whimper of a puppy at night, and the temptation to go and cuddle and comfort it will be very strong. Try to ignore it as the puppy will be quite used to being alone within a week. There are times, however, when I would recommend keeping your dog company – such as during particularly violent thunderstorms. Some animals can ignore thunder completely, but others become hysterical and need the sense of security provided by company on such occasions.

everything that is taught will be remembered. Watching a mother with her litter is the best way of understanding the disciplining of dogs. She will stand for no nosense. If a particularly plucky puppy gets out of hand and ignores its mother she will snap quite nastily at it until it stops and then comfort it if it cries. If a puppy is pestering her she will warn it to stop by growling, and the next time the puppy will associate this sound with disapproval, stopping immediately. Eventually it will learn which activities cause the angry sounds and cease to do them all together. With a human owner the same pattern works whether it is being taught something basic or slightly more complicated and whether it is required to stop doing something or learn a rule, for if it is encouraged to do a trick and is rewarded for performing it successfully, it will continue to do it. Tone of voice is of vital importance and things of pleasure must not be linked with a disapproving sound. Its name should always signify pleasure when it is called and if its name is used in association with scolding it will quickly associate the two. It must also be remembered that dogs will think they are being punished or rewarded for an activity that has just been done or is going on. If a dog is called over and punished for chewing the carpet it will immediately think that what it did wrong was to respond when its name was called, rather than ruining the carpet.

Training should begin as soon as a puppy is brought into the home. The basics are toilet training, teaching it its name, the word 'no', sitting down when told to, accustoming it to a collar and lead, walking to heel and to come immediately when called. If training is consistent and the tone used firm but gentle, with sessions that are mutually enjoyable, there is a good chance of success when training a dog, whatever its breed.

'It's a Dog's Life'

These days, when dogs enjoy a comfortable and comparatively lazy existence, that popular phrase has little relevance when talking about the day to day life of a dog. It dates back to the days when the dog was employed by man in a variety of jobs, often for very little return. The switching of roles from the dog as a working animal to the dog as a pet is largely an event of the 20th century. In many spheres where dogs were employed industralisation has displaced them; motorised transport now moves flocks of sheep from the larger farms to market, and mechanical alarm systems now fulfil the duties that were once performed by a ferocious guard dog, especially in urban areas. But the working days of the dog are far from over. New uses are continually being found by man for his faithful canine friend, and

Large, trusting, clear and bright – a dog's eyes are probably its most attractive feature. The eyes need to be carefully looked after and, if possible, checked every day. Any discharge coming from the eye should be reported to the vet. If the eye looks irritated (usually indicated by watering) it should be bathed in a mild saline solution – but boil the water before you add the salt.

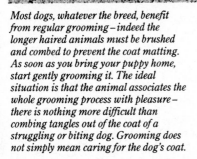

there are many situations where a dog does the work so well, and provides such protection or friendship, that it is unlikely ever to be replaced.

All working dogs are trained to a very high standard. The abilities that top class sheep dogs display at trials are made even more remarkable when it is remembered that their wild instincts tell tham to kill these animals for food, not to protect them. But these dogs, amongst which the elegant Border collie reigns supreme, have been bred with the herding instinct in them. As early as three months of age a Border collie pup may show the instinct to round things up. The work expected from a sheepdog varies according to the surrounding countryside. Some will be working on flat land, maneouvring the sheep inside pens, whilst others will be trained to gather the flock from up in the hills, bringing it down to the valleys where the shepherds

Most dogs, whatever the breed, benefit from regular grooming – indeed the longer haired animals must be brushed and combed to prevent the coat matting. As soon as you bring your puppy home, start gently grooming it. The ideal situation is that the animal associates the whole grooming process with pleasure – there is nothing more difficult than combing tangles out of the coat of a struggling or biting dog. Grooming does not simply mean caring for the dog's coat.

Like humans, their teeth need cleaning – a job which can be done using an ordinary toothbrush, and their nails need clipping, although walking on a hard surface will keep them fairly short.
I would suggest having the dog's nails clipped by a vet as they have a living quick growing down the centre and it is easy to cut this by mistake, causing considerable pain to the animal, and perhaps even destroying its trust in you.

are waiting. Stamina is of the utmost importance – thirty or forty miles may easily be covered in a working day, sometimes on very rugged ground.

The two main breeds used as guide dogs for the blind are Labradors and golden retrievers. In their work they display not only to

just how high a standard it is possible to train a dog but also how patient and loyal dogs can be. They take the initiative on so many occasions that it is almost possible to believe that their owners can see, so sure are they of the lead their dogs are taking. Most of the dogs picked for training are females and, as with all specialised dogs, have to be selected very carefully. Because the association that exists between these dogs and their owners is unique, the personality of the prospective owner must also be assessed so that the partnership is as complementary as possible. The owner must have a strong desire to be independent and it is vital that he or she is physically active as this will be an aid in learning how to handle the dog correctly and forming the strong bond which is so important. During the working life of a guide dog, which is normally about nine years, the animal will steer its owners around obstacles, across roads and along busy streets.

The police dog is another familiar working animal. The most popular breed is the alsatian, and each dog is expected to perform a variety of duties, from catching criminals to sniffing out drugs. The best age for training, which requires great patience and skill, is considered to be between twelve and eighteen months, and each dog has one particular handler whose every command, however slight it may appear to be, it must obey. The training often involves teaching the dogs to go against many instinctive desires, for instance if a dog catches a criminal it must learn to release its hold instantly on command and not get excited by the struggle which will invariably follow. It must also lose any inhibitions it may have acquired to bite, which any highly trained dog will be reluctant to do. If a trained police dog smells an item of clothing which has been worn by a person it will be able to follow the scent for miles. Ben, a black Labrador, was famous in the police force for making over one hundred arrests, while the

As this delightful photograph shows, bonds of friendship regularly exist between dogs of different ages and breeds, although if you possess a fully-grown dog and intend to buy a puppy, be careful not to pay too much attention to the new arrival lest the older animal feel jealous or left out.

world's top tracking dog is 'Trep' who works for Florida's Dade County Crime Force. Trep has sniffed out over 35 million pounds worth of drugs.

Popular Breeds

Large, small, docile or excitable, very intelligent and sometimes extremely daft – there are as many different kinds of dogs as there are human beings. Not all dog-owners will necessarily love all dogs, owning a toy poodle as opposed to a Great Dane is probably as different as owning a cat instead of a horse. Many cartoons have humorously portrayed dog-owners who look exactly like their dogs, from the clothes they wear to the hairstyles they adopt, and others are quick to point out that some will choose dogs that are an extension of their own personalities.

Many of the rare breeds of dog are beautiful to look at but exepensive to buy. It is often thought, usually wrongly, that they require a lot more care and attention and have especially unpredictable temperaments. So it is apparent that for a

A clean, well looked-after dog is a constant source of pleasure, and apart from brushing and combing, most dogs will benefit from the occasional bath. I find that the easiest way to wash a dog is to stand it in a bath which has a shower attachment. Dogs hate being washed in cold water, so make sure that the water is coming through warm before you wet the animal. Shampoo and thoroughly rinse the body before you wash the head – and while washing the head, avoid the eyes as shampoo really stings them, and keep water away from the sensitive insides of the ears. Dry the dog briskly with a thick towel and keep it warm while it dries.

1

2

3

companion or good family dog certain breeds are firm favourites. Among the toy breeds the Yorkshire terriers are especially popular. Sweet in appearance and full of charm, these little dogs are affectionately called 'toughies' because of their remarkable courage. Many is the Yorkie owner who has had to rescue his little friend after it has picked a fight with a dog several times larger than itself, apparently forgetting the limitations of its own size. They are capable of great affection, but a word of warning regarding other people's hutch pets is necessary. Their ratting instincts are very strong – one farmer who owned a Yorkie in Devon had to keep his rabbit hutches far above the ground to keep his dog from injuring them, but this is the exception rather than the rule. In urban areas these desires are quelled and Yorkies make delightful and devoted pets.

Toy poodles were developed at the beginning of this century but the standard poodle dates back much further in time. There is also a larger size which can stand as high as an alsatian. Their popularity can be attributed to their attractive appearance and tremendous sense of fun. They are intelligent and usually friendly, ready to lick most hands that are gently offered to them. However, if anybody gets on the wrong side of a poodle, it may feel that its benevolent nature has been abused and winning its affection afterwards could prove a difficult task.

Possibly the most noble looking of all dogs, the German shepherd dog, or alsatian, is intelligent, highly adaptable and extremely versatile, which explains why it is such a popular working dog. But despite its imposing nature and tendency to be a 'one man dog' alsatians are very popular as pets. They are reliable, active and very protective of their owners and their owner's property, particularly if a good, trusting relationship has been established. If these dogs are mismanaged it must be admitted that

Very young puppies like these (6) keep snuggled up together for warmth, comfort and the sense of security that company gives. They need to eat frequently and sleep for long periods at a time. Puppies can start eating solids at about four to six weeks, and at eight weeks (not before) they are ready to go to their new owners.

1

2

3

4

5

7

they can be fairly menacing and this is why strangers often find them off-hand, but they are essentially friendly and passionately devoted dogs.

Labradors are lovely. They look cuddly, gentle, even-tempered and patient, and none of these bely their nature. It is not always recommended that any puppy should be brought into the home if there are very young children, but if this must be done, few dogs would fit the bill better. Black or golden they are fun-loving, obliging dogs who lavish affection on everybody. Not easily ruffled, Labradors will only get aggressive as a last resort and even then it will only be a warning growl. As with all dogs it is essential to give them exercise. These particular dogs were bred to retrieve game for their handlers after a shoot and this urge to 'fetch and carry' will still be there, even in the most home-loving of Labradors, so if there is a puppy in the house, hide those new shoes away. If they are shut up on their own for a long time they are liable to become bored and destructive to property.

The beautiful Irish setters, often called red setters because of the colour of the coat, are notorious for their mischievous nature. In play, whichever way a setter appears to be about to run, it will invariably double back when you get close and go streaking off in a different direction and stand, apparently laughing at you from a distance. Very few setters can be called reliable and, like Labradors, if they don't want to hear their name being called it is as if they are deaf. They are also very headstrong when they are on a lead and will quite happily drag their owner off in a variety of directions despite loud protestations, and any attempt to scold them proves fruitless. Nevertheless they are devoted to their owners and are open and friendly to most people, displaying little aggression, even when teased.

There are, of course, numerous other popular breeds, boxers, bull terriers, collies and mongrels, all with their own distinct personalities. Whatever their shape or size, dogs are among the greatest companions man has ever, or will ever have.

me of the most popular breeds of dog are featured on
se pages:
Graceful and elegant Afghan Hounds need a lot of
ooming and exercise.
Spotted Dalmations are very friendly animals whose
tractive short coats need little grooming.
The pretty Papillon or Butterfly Dog is a member of
Toy Spaniel family. Its coat is long and silky and its
ears are large and heavily fringed.
(4) One of the most appealing of all young dogs must
surely be the Golden Cocker Spaniel puppy. This friendly
dog has a sunny nature and makes a delightful playmate.
(5) The highly popular Collie.
(6) A mournful-eyed Saint Bernard.
(7) The endearing Yellow Labrador.
(8) The beautiful, gentle Golden Retriever.

First English edition published in 1981 by Colour Library International Ltd.
This edition is published by Crescent Books, Distributed by Crown Publishers Inc.
Illustrations and text ©: Colour Library International Ltd. 163 East 64th Street, New York 10021.
Colour separations by FERCROM, Barcelona, Spain.
Display and text filmsetting by Focus Photoset, London, England.
Printed and bound in Barcelona, Spain by JISA-RIEUSSET & EUROBINDER.
All rights reserved.
Library of Congress Catalog Card Number: 81-67586
CRESCENT 1981